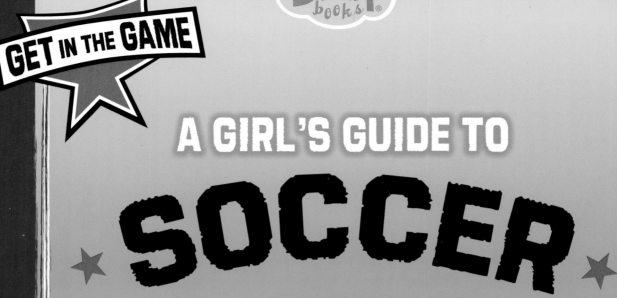

GET IN THE GAME

Snap books

A GIRL'S GUIDE TO

SOCCER

by Allyson Valentine Schrier

Consultant:
Tracy Noonan
Dynasty Goalkeeping
Carrboro, North Carolina

CAPSTONE PRESS
a capstone imprint

Snap Books are published by Capstone Press,
1710 Roe Crest Drive, North Mankato, Minnesota 56003
www.capstonepub.com

Books published by Capstone Press are manufactured with paper
containing at least 10 percent post-consumer waste.

Library of Congress Cataloging-in-Publication Data
Schrier, Allyson Valentine.
  A girl's guide to soccer / by Allyson Valentine Schrier.
     p. cm. — (Snap books. Get in the game.)
  Includes index.
  Summary: "Quizzes, rules, and tips and tricks on how to play soccer"—Provided by publisher.
  ISBN 978-1-4296-7671-7 (library binding)
  1. Soccer for girls—Juvenile literature. I. Title. II. Series.

  GV944.2.S35 2012
  796.334—dc23   2011034041

Editor: Mari Bolte
Designer: Bobbie Nuytten
Media Researcher: Eric Gohl
Production Specialist: Kathy McColley

Photo Credits:
BigStockPhoto/jaboardm, 9, R.W. Hunter, 12; Capstone Studio/Karon Dubke, 5 (bottom), 15, 17, 19, 21,
22, 23, 27, 29; Getty Images/The Image Bank/Ron Levine, cover (left); iStockphoto/Kirk Strickland, 6, 8,
10, 14, Stephen Pell, 11; Shutterstock/Africa Studio, 24 (right), Anke van Wyk, 24 (left), creativedoxfoto,
13, Le Do, cover (right), back cover, 2, 4–5 (top), 7 (top), Melinda Fawver, 25 (top), SunnyS, 25 (bottom),
Teerasak, 7 (bottom)

Design Elements
Shutterstock/Albachiaraa (grass), Sergey Kandakov (stars),
Solid (cheering crowd)

Printed in the United States of America in North Mankato, Minnesota.
042013   007262R

TABLE OF CONTENTS

CHAPTER 1 ★

How Much Do You Know?

Could you kick a soccer ball before you could walk? Or is the urge to chase a ball around a grassy field something new for you? Maybe you'd rather cheer for your favorite team from the sidelines. Whatever your reasons for loving the sport, you're not alone—soccer is the most popular sport in the world!

Even though it's been played for thousands of years, the game hasn't changed much. Soccer is still played by two teams, each trying to kick the ball into a goal. The team that scores the most goals wins. Think you know a lot about soccer? Take this quiz to test your soccer IQ.

1. With your speed, great ball handling skills, and accuracy at firing balls into the goal, you are right at home playing:
- a) midfielder
- b) forward
- c) goalkeeper
- d) sweeper

2. With most of the team dressed alike, it's hard to keep track of how many players are on the field. How many team members can play at the same time?
- a) 9
- b) 10
- c) 11
- d) 13

3. Which of these is not a position on the soccer field?
- a) midfielder
- b) striker
- c) sweeper
- d) duster

4. Your opponents took a shot on your goal. While blocking the shot, your defender knocked the ball out over your own end line. The other team gets to take a:

a) penalty shot

c) corner kick

b) throw in

d) goal kick

5. When a player dashes down the field controlling the soccer ball with tiny taps of her feet she is:

a) dribbling

c) bounding

b) dabbling

d) tapping

6. During a soccer game, a player gets a yellow card when she:

a) scores the most goals.

b) kicks the ball farther than anyone else.

c) is being warned by the referee for being too rough.

d) has kicked the ball out of bounds more than three times.

7. Unlike the other girls on the team, the goalkeeper is allowed to stop the ball with her:

a) head

b) stomach

c) thighs

d) hands

8. In soccer, play is stopped when:

a) Someone scores a goal.

b) The ball goes out of bounds.

c) A penalty occurs.

d) All of the above.

9. Your teammate is wide open with no defender in sight. You want to send her a perfect pass. What part of your foot should you not use to kick the ball?

a) the top of your foot

b) the inside of your foot

c) your toes

d) the outside of your foot

10. Nice shot! Too bad you missed. The ball rolled over the other team's end line. What happens now?

a) The other team gets to take a corner kick.

b) The other team gets to take a penalty kick.

c) The other team gets a goal kick.

d) You get to take a throw in.

for the answers, see page 31

CHAPTER 2

The Basics

Your team is geared up and ready to go. You've laced up your **cleats**, pulled up your socks, and slipped on your shin guards. The goalkeeper uses gloves to help her catch the ball. It's time to take your positions and get things rolling.

Places, Everyone!

Soccer has four basic positions. Give each one a try! You may find a hidden talent. And playing every position is the best way to really understand both the game and your teammates.

EAT: a shoe with small ber spikes on the bottom help soccer players stop or n quickly

Each team has four defenders (D), four midfielders (M), two strikers (S), and a goalie (G).

FORWARDS If you're fast and skilled with the ball, then offense is where you belong. Use your head, legs, torso, and feet to get the ball toward the other team's goal. With extra speed and surefire aim, you could play striker. The striker is a superstar forward who stays close to the other team's goal. A striker's main job is to rack up the goals.

MIDFIELDER: Can't decide whether you'd be better playing offense or defense? Be a midfielder and do it all! Midfielders pass the ball upfield to the forwards. They also stop the ball before it gets near the goal. This is the place for girls who like to run!

DEFENDER: A team made of 11 forwards would never win a game. Somebody needs stay by the goal. Use your defensive skills and solid kick to keep your opponents from scoring. Keep close to your opponents, and try to get the ball away from them. With practice, you could play sweeper. The sweeper's job is to stay back and cover for the other defenders. If the other team gets through the other defenders, the sweeper is there to provide backup.

Other defenders include center backs and outside backs. Center backs track the other team's forwards and midfielders and try to steal the ball. Outside backs keep the other team's forwards away from the goal. Without defenders, the other team would have easy access to the goal.

GOALKEEPER: Can you handle the pressure of one-on-one showdowns with attacking forwards? Can you shake it off when a ball makes it past you? Do you have the courage, the agility, and the catlike reflexes needed to stop a shot? Then step in front of the goal and get ready to run, jump, and dive to guard the goal.

The goalkeeper can touch the ball with her hands, but only within the 18-yard (16.5-meter) box around the goal.

Let's Play!

Every player is in position. The referee blows the whistle. It's nearly nonstop action on the field for 40 minutes. If you're watching a college or pro game, the halves will be 45 minutes long. Play halts when someone scores, when the ball goes out of bounds, or if there's a penalty. Coaches use those pauses in the game to make player substitutions so everyone gets game time. After a 10-minute halftime break, the teams switch sides, and the game continues.

Protecting the Net

You can use three different tackle styles to get the ball from the other player. The most simple is the block tackle. A player from each team tries to kick the ball at the same time. The defender uses her forward motion to stop the ball. The motion should cause your opponent to trip or lose possession of the ball.

To do a poke tackle, the defender runs alongside of the player with the ball. Just after the other player has just touched the ball, the defender steps in front of the other player and "pokes" the ball away.

A slide tackle is used as a last resort. The defender slides feet-first at an angle toward the ball. If the tackle is done right, the other player loses control of the ball. But if the tackler misses, there may be no other defenders nearby to stop the other team. And if the tackle is done poorly, you may get a penalty.

Scoring to Win

The midfielder sends you a perfect pass. You dribble upfield, dodging defenders. It's a face-off between you and the goalkeeper. You fake left, dart to the right, and slam the ball into the net. Goal! The crowd goes wild. People are still cheering as both teams line up again. This time, the other team kicks off.

Out of Bounds

That big rectangle of grass may feel huge when you're running back and forth. But that can change when you're trying to keep the ball inbounds. How the ball comes back to the field depends on how it rolled out.

If your teammate kicked the ball over the sideline, the other team throws the ball in. They throw it from the point at which the ball left the field.

Say the other team tried to score a goal. The goalkeeper blocked the shot, but your defender accidentally kicked the ball over the end line. Her kick means the other team gets to take a kick from the corner arc.

Now it's your team's turn to score. But the shot missed and rolled over the other team's goal line. Your opponent's goalkeeper gets to take a goal kick. She must kick the ball into play from the top edge of the 6-yard (5.5-m) box. The ball must travel to a player outside the 18-yard (16.5-m) box.

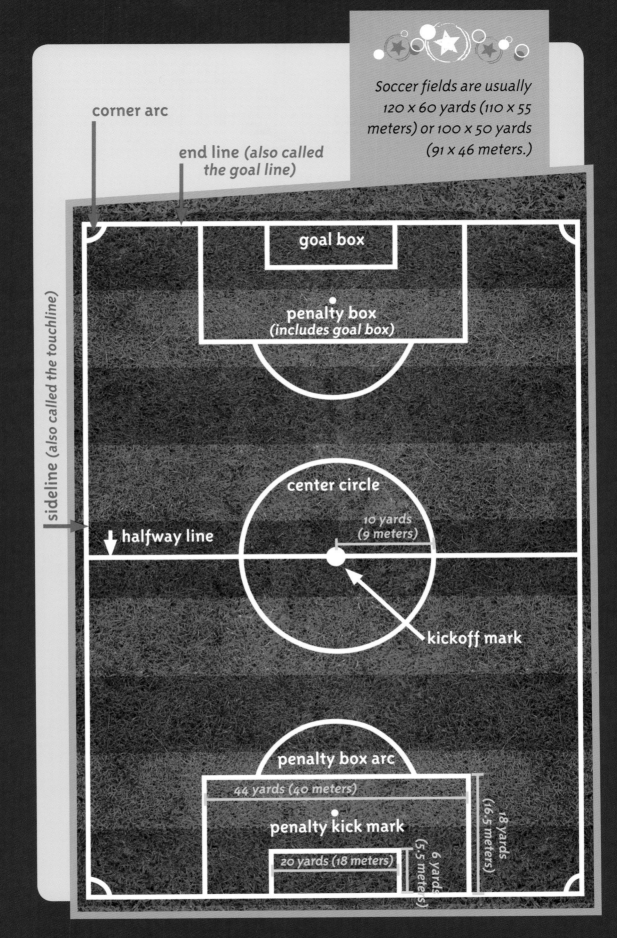

corner arc

end line *(also called the goal line)*

Soccer fields are usually 120 x 60 yards (110 x 55 meters) or 100 x 50 yards (91 x 46 meters.)

sideline *(also called the touchline)*

goal box

penalty box
(includes goal box)

center circle

10 yards
(9 meters)

halfway line

kickoff mark

penalty box arc

44 yards (40 meters)

penalty kick mark

18 yards
(16.5 meters)

20 yards (18 meters)

6 yards
(5.5 meters)

Penalties

Rough play and handballs are just two of the fouls that stop play. A free kick is awarded when a penalty occurs outside the 18-yard (16.5-m) box. During a free kick, your opponents must be 30 feet (9 m) away. The players can't get close to challenge for the ball until the ball has been kicked. There are two kinds of free kicks—direct and indirect. A direct kick can score a goal right away. Multiple players must touch an indirect kick before it can score a goal.

A penalty kick happens when a foul is made inside the box. The other team gets a free one-on-one shot with your goalkeeper. The ball must start 36 feet (11 m) from the goal. And the keeper can't leave the goal line until the ball is kicked.

Get too rough, and you could wind up with a yellow card. Two of those, or one very serious case of rough play, and you will be shown a red card. Then you're out of the game! A red card is a big deal, and not just for you. Your team can't replace the red-carded player. They must continue playing the game while down a player. So be good sports and focus on having fun, not on playing rough.

Only One Winner

The team with the most goals wins. But what if the score is tied? If your league doesn't allow ties, there will be two overtime periods to determine a winner. If the score is still tied, then it's time for sudden death. The coaches choose five skilled players to take a single, high-pressure penalty shot on goal. Still tied? Get ready for a sudden victory round of penalty shots where the first team to score wins the game.

Whether you win or lose, good sportsmanship is important when playing the game.

CHAPTER 3 ★

Soccer Does a Body Good!

Soccer is not only fun, it's good for you! Those long runs up and down the field are a terrific workout. It's great for your heart, lungs, muscles, and even your brain.

Soccer also scores points for being a super weight-bearing exercise. This type of exercise allows your body to fight gravity while you play. Working against gravity triggers your body to make more bone tissue for strong bones. And those shifts between walking, running, starting, and stopping help strengthen bones even more.

Earn What You Eat

Girls on the go have more muscle and less fat than girls who don't exercise. Walking, breathing, and brushing your teeth all burn **calories**. But the calories burned don't come close to the number you burn playing soccer. When you play soccer regularly, your body's **metabolism** increases. So even on days when you don't have practice you still burn off more calories.

CALORIE: a measurement of the amount of energy that food gives you

METABOLISM: the process of changing food into energy

EDIBLE SOCCER BALLS ★

Looking for something tasty to eat that is both great for your body and fun to eat? Get the girls together to make this sweet and oh-so-good peanut butter treat.

INGREDIENTS

½ cup (120 milliliters) peanut butter

½ cup (120 mL) honey

½ teaspoon (2.5 mL) vanilla

½ teaspoon (2.5 mL) cinnamon

2 cups (480 mL) crispy brown rice cereal (or other puffed cereal)

¼ cup (60 mL) chocolate chips

¼ cup (60 mL) white chocolate chips

SUPPLIES

microwave-safe bowl

spoon

large plate

parchment paper

Step 1: Place peanut butter, honey, vanilla, and cinnamon in the microwave-safe bowl.

Step 2: Microwave peanut butter mixture for 30 seconds and then stir. Continue microwaving and stirring until the mixture is thin enough to stir easily.

Step 3: Add rice cereal, chocolate chips, and white chocolate chips. Stir well.

Step 4: Cover plate with parchment paper.

Step 5: Roll cereal and peanut butter mixture into small balls. Place balls on plate.

Step 6: Press extra chocolate chips into the balls, to copy the pattern on real soccer balls.

Step 7: Store peanut butter balls in the refrigerator until firm.

Soccer Works Your Brain

Soccer players use their noggins for more than **headers**. They also use them to decide what play to try next. All that quick-thinking helps your brain work smarter both on and off the field. It's a fact that girls who stay active do better in school. Soccer also helps build self-esteem, beat depression, and boost self-confidence. Even if your team loses a game, you'll still feel like a winner.

Soccer Teaches Skills for Life

Soccer is a commitment. Miss a practice and you might miss a valuable drill. Skip a game and your whole team suffers. Being part of a team teaches self-discipline and social skills. These skills help you shine in the classroom, within your family, and someday at a job. And life is brighter with friends. Making new friends is the best part about being on a team!

Play Safe, Play Smart!

Like any sport, soccer comes with risks. You might knock heads with another player while going for the ball. A quick turn could lead to a twisted ankle or pulled muscle. There's always a risk of getting hit with a sloppy slide tackle. Studies show that girls are four to six times more likely than boys to get hurt playing soccer. This fact may be because of a hormone called **estrogen**. Some scientists believe that estrogen loosens girls' **ligaments**, making injuries more likely.

HEADER: a shot where players use their heads to hit the ball

ESTROGEN: a hormone produced only by females

LIGAMENT: band of tissue that connects or supports bones and joints

Make sure you're feeling good before the game. Get a good night's sleep and drink plenty of water. Twice as many injuries happen in the second half of the game. Tired players make mistakes. If you're not feeling fresh, ask the coach to put in a substitute so you can recharge. If you're injured, give your body a rest. It's better to miss one game than an entire season. Remember to stretch well before and after the game. A proper warm-up and good nutrition go a long way toward preventing injury.

★ CHAPTER 4 ★

Better, Stronger, and Faster

A defender needs energy to outrun forwards charging toward the goal. And a forward running on empty can't skirt past a pile of midfielders. Even a goalkeeper will lose focus if she's not fueled up right. For maximum energy, soccer girls need a winning combination. They need to eat and drink the right foods at the right time.

Before the Game

You've got a belly full of butterflies before the game. But don't let that keep you from eating. Three to four hours before you hit the field, grab a healthy snack to keep your energy up. Complex **carbohydrates**, such as whole wheat pasta, cereal and grains, or brown rice and beans are great choices.

CARBOHYDRATE: a substance that gives you energy

Complex carbs provide long-lasting energy and give your muscles what they need to work. So snack on a PB and J on whole wheat. Make yourself a grilled chicken salad with light dressing. Grab a bowl of pasta or cereal. Even fruits, 100-percent juices, and dairy products are sources of complex carbs. Choose them before digging into processed foods, such as cookies, candy, or french fries.

Tip: Follow the 80 percent rule: Eat until you are almost full. Overeating before a game will slow you down.

During The Game

Your muscles tire and your **endurance** drops when your body runs out of water. So drink early and often. Drinking water before practice speeds up the rate your body sweats. And sweat is a good thing! It's nature's way of keeping you from overheating. Start drinking water about two hours before the game. Drink 1 ounce (0.28 grams) of water for every 10 pounds (4.5 kilograms) of body weight. And don't drink it all at once—guzzling a lot of water will only give you a stomachache.

If you get hungry during the game, munch watery fruit such as orange slices, watermelon, and grapes.

Wondering what to drink? Water is great, but on really hot days, sports drinks can be better. These fluids are packed with carbohydrates and **electrolytes**. But avoid drinks with caffeine. They won't help your performance and can make you jumpy. Steer clear of drinks with high-fructose corn syrup and other added sugars. They add empty calories that will only give you short-term energy.

ENDURANCE: the ability to keep doing an activity for long periods of time

ELECTROLYTE: a mineral that encourages the body to drink more water

After the Game

You may not feel hungry after the game, but your body needs nutrients to help your muscles recover. The sooner you eat and drink, the less likely you are to feel sore. Water, fresh fruit, and a protein-packed snack, such as cheese, trail mix, or salted nuts, would do the trick. And as much as you might want an ice-cold soda, skip it. The bubbles will trick your stomach into thinking it's full before your body gets all the liquid you need to recover.

Tip: You may be surprised to hear that a glass of chocolate milk is a great post-game drink. It's the perfect mixture of carbs, protein, and fat to help your body resupply itself. Make milk moustaches cool again!

CHAPTER 5 ★

Fun Off the Field

Soccer isn't just about kicking a ball around and scoring goals. It's also about working as a team. The more you know about your teammates, the better you'll work together on the field. You'll get to know each others' likes and dislikes and strengths and weaknesses. Teamwork is best when it happens year-round and on and off the field.

During the soccer season, take the time to bond. Choose a psych-up song for your team and sing it together. Paint your nails in team colors. Help each other dress up ponytails or braids with team-colored ribbons.

There's no bad time to bond! After the season is over, help your team stay in good soccer shape. Gather for a group run. Try out some new skills and drills. Challenge another team to a friendly scrimmage. Or head to a tennis court with your favorite soccer ball and try out a game of soccer-tennis! Anything that will keep your **coordination** sharp will help your game.

Don't limit yourself to soccer stuff. Meet at a bowling alley, the movies, or the swimming pool. As a group, go watch your local women's college or pro team play. Start a team blog that tells the world that you are some serious soccer girls.

COORDINATION: the ability to control body movements

Soccer is a friend for life. Just take a look at the teams of ladies playing well into their senior years! And why not? Soccer keeps you fit and makes you stronger. It boosts your self-esteem and confidence. And best of all, it helps you meet girls who share your love of soccer.

TEAM SPIRIT POM HAT ★

Even when the soccer season is over, you can show off your team spirit with these sporty pom hats!

WHAT YOU'LL NEED:

measuring tape

¾ yard (0.7 m) piece of fleece fabric

scissors

fabric glue

pencil

12-inch (30-centimeter) long, ½ inch (1.3 cm) wide strip of fleece fabric in a different color

beads

Step 1: Measure the length around your head. Add 1 inch (2.5 cm) to the measurement.

Step 2: Gently tug the large piece fleece in both directions. It will be stretchier one way than the other. Cut a rectangle that is 30 inches (76 cm) long. Make sure your cuts go the non-stretchy way.

Step 3: Cutting the opposite direction, trim the rectangle to the measurement you took in step 1.

Step 4: Fold the fabric lengthwise. Glue the edges together to make a long, narrow tube. Let dry.

Step 5: Measure and mark a line 4 ½ inches (11 cm) from each end of the tube. Cut fringe strips ½ an inch wide at each end of the tube, stopping at the pencil line.

Step 6: Turn the tube inside out until the fringed ends come together. Tie the 12-inch-long strip of fleece tightly below the fringed ends.

Step 7: Fold the bottom of the hat up, to make a brim. If desired, tie beads onto the fleece strip.

GLOSSARY

calorie (KA-luh-ree)—a measurement of the amount of energy that food gives you

carbohydrate (kar-boh-HYE-drate)—a substance found in foods such as bread, rice, cereal, and potatoes that gives you energy

cleat (KLEET)—a shoe with small tips on the bottom to help soccer players stop or turn quickly

coordination (koh-OR-duh-nay-shun)—the ability to control body movements

electrolyte (i-lek-TRAH-lyte)—a mineral that encourages the body to drink more water; electrolytes contain an electric charge

endurance (en-DUR-enss)—the ability to keep doing an activity for long periods of time

estrogen (es-TRUH-juhn)—a hormone produced only by females

header (HED-ur)—a technique where players use their heads to hit the ball

ligament (lig-UH-mehnt)—a band of tissue that connects or supports bones and joints

metabolism (muh-TAB-uh-liz-uhm)—the process of changing food into energy

READ MORE

Bazemore, Suzanne. *Soccer: How It Works*. The Science of Sports. Mankato, Minn.: Capstone Press, 2010.

Forest, Christopher. *Play Soccer Like a Pro: Key Skills and Tips*. Play Like a Pro. Mankato, Minn.: Capstone Press, 2011.

Gifford, Clive. *The Inside Story of Soccer*. Sports World. New York: Rosen Central, 2012.

Rediger, Pat. *Soccer*. In The Zone. New York: Weigl Publishers, 2010.

INTERNET SITES

FactHound offers a safe, fun way to find Internet sites related to this book. All of the sites on FactHound have been researched by our staff.

Here's all you do:

Visit *www.facthound.com*

Type in this code: 9781429676717

Check out projects, games and lots more at
www.capstonekids.com

QUIZ ANSWERS: 1. b 2. c 3. d 4. c 5. a 6. c 7. d 8. d 9. b 10. c

INDEX